"All I have is praise—praise for the life, the good, rich, full life, in beautiful words. For the sacred and the doubt that go hand in hand, for the love, the joy, the pain transcended, for the amazement, the sense of wonder... It's wonderful."

— Grace Schulman, author, and winner of The Frost Medal
for Distinguished Lifetime Achievement in American Poetry

"I am not much of a poetry reader these days because so much of what is published seems to me self-congratulatory and obscure all at once, as if written in some sort of private language, without shape or music. To the many readers who feel as I do, Bill Henderson's *The Family Bible* will come as a shock and a surprise. These poems, often no more than a dozen lines, never more than a couple of sparsely filled pages, carry a distinct punch, and are always crystal clear. They are funny, moving, occasionally bitter or blasphemous, but always intensely alive and communicative. Bill is a man of faith who sometimes struggles with it, but whose feelings for family, friends, even the human race, are transparent. I read the book straight through, almost unheard of in a poetry reader, and I think a lot of people will want to do the same: it's that refreshing."

— John Baker, former editor-in-chief of *Publishers Weekly*

"Wielding irony with dexterity, Henderson cuts through the claptrap, threats, and barbarity to uncover the quiet, compassionate God who got left behind. This is a brave, illuminating, and highly engaging book."

— Joan Murray, author of *Dancing On The Edge*
and other poetry collections

"A rare statement of faith: bracing, astringent, cleansing, and genuine... *The Family Bible* should be a companion volume to Bible classes all over the country, right next to Paine's *Age of Reason*."

— Reverend Rob McCall
Blue Hill, Maine Congregational Church

THE FAMILY BIBLE

poems

Bill Henderson

PUSHCART

Designed by Mary Kornblum

Cover illustration from Grant Wood's painting
The Midnight Ride of Paul Revere

Published by Pushcart Press
P.O. Box 380
Wainscott, New York 11975

Distributed by W.W. Norton & Company, Inc
500 Fifth Avenue
New York, New York 10110

Printed in The United States of America

ISBN 978 0 9600 9777 7

Paperback edition published in association with
Black Mountain Press, Asheville, North Carolina

for
Bob, Ruth, William and Hunter

TABLE
OF
CONTENTS

FAITH

I wanted to be
An atheist
But I lost
My faith.

After brain surgery
My brother's wife was
Cancer free.

Young mother, artist
kind, funny,

Now half-bodied,
Semi-brained,
Cancer free.

DEBBY

Bob slept on the floor
Next to her shell.
"Debby's still in there,"
He said.

Bathed her,
Changed her diapers,
Fed her with a spoon.

Didn't ask God why.

For twenty-two years
He slept on hardwood
Next to her.

Buried her Bible with
Her cancer-free ashes.

In Sunday School
We kids loved the story of
The odd animals,
Two by two,
The big boat Noah built,
The stormy voyage.

NOAH

After the genocide
God painted a pretty rainbow
Over a corpse strewn sea.

Our teachers didn't tell us
How kids drown.
First they descend,
Flail upwards to the light,
Thrash about,
Call for mom
Descend again,
Rise,
Tire,
It's like falling asleep.
Listening to
A good story.

On the morning
Pop said his prayers, slept
And died, I hiked
The Appian Way.
Once a chariot path, now
A miles long, gasoline fumed
Traffic jam.

For hours I slogged on
Towards the catacombs and
The remains of the
Cowering faithful
Paul wrote love letters to
Thousands of years ago.

ROME

A grumpy priest led me
Down into the hole
Where they had worshipped.
I saw skulls, bones,
Climbed into the Spring air
To find another love letter
At American Express.
"Call home urgent. Mom."

If you are a young pilgrim
In Rome and your father
Dies suddenly
You:
Laugh congratulations to him.
His Jesus took a gentle man
Gently.
"You did it Pop"!

You:
Try prayer, but
Forget how to or
Who to.

You:
Open the Word of God
In a Protestant church
But find too many words of God.

You:
Prowl ancient Catholic churches
With blank-eyed statues
Giggling school girls at confession
And bloody hanging corpses.

You:
Ask a priest to pray for Pop.
"And he was a Catholic, are you?"
You reach out to the priest,
Hold his arm,
Spanning the gap he just named.
"No."
"Of course I will pray for him."
He smiles tightly, sending you
and Pop to hell.

You:
Alone in a hotel room
With a pint of bourbon
For the first time
You cry.

A still small voice.
I KINGS 19:12

THE PHOTO

On the Greek beach
A still small corpse,
About five years old,
Neatly dressed,
Head resting on the sand,
As if napping,
The tide tugging at his shoes
His boat gone,
Parents too.

His photo spoke a holy voice,
Too quiet for the
Holy fanatics to hear.
He shouted to the world
Before we returned to
Our daily racket.

16

THE GREAT COMMANDMENTS

Comfort your Pathetic Parents
Romp with your Funny Friends
Remember the Heaven you just left
Before you forget.

THE BEATITUDES

Blessed are they who are constantly amazed
       As the moon rises.
Blessed are they who dance
       Before they can walk.
Blessed are they who kiss
       Without asking for a kiss
Blessed are they who feel the hamster's pain
       Before their own.
Blessed are they who are proud
       To be a girl.
Blessed are they who laugh
       Because farts are hilarious.
Blessed are they who remember Wordsworth's
       "Trailing clouds of glory do we come
       from God."
Blessed are they for whom love is
       As real as a rock.

WEEPING GOD

Debby was a God-mutt,
Jewish dad,
Catholic mom.

In 458 BC Ezra threw
Such mutts out
Of Israel,
To starve,
Or whatever.

Maybe that's why
God allowed her to
Become a cancer-free shell?

The tv minister says God
Lets bad things happen
To good people, but He
Weeps with us...

But oh weeping God,
Debby was a loyal mutt,
Ate your Jesus as best she could,
A trained nun brought Him weekly,
Hand fed her.

Is there mercy in Your tears?
What's the use of Your tears?
Is there a theologian in the house?

Thou shalt not suffer a witch to live.
EXODUS 22:18

QUESTIONS FOR COTTON

Salem, 1692

My mistress named me Prudence.
I didn't weigh enough to
Break my hairy neck
So I am just hanging around
On this shining pile.

Fourteen witches,
Five wizards,
And us two dogs
Bagged by the righteous
Reverend Mather.

They said I
Peed on petunias
Pirouetted in poop
And probed my privates
In public.

"Devil Dog!"
They wrote me up.
(You can look it up)
Me and this puppy,
Patience.

Side by side we dangle,
Trying to howl,
Desperate to pant.
Nearby Purity,
My mistress,
In chains,
Waits her turn
On the rope.
She loved me too much
Said Rev. Mather.

Around us:
Savages,
Quakers,
Papists,
The French,
The forever forest.

Rev. Mather,
Did you have
To take God
So seriously?

And I will kill her children with death.
REVELATION 2:23

BREAKFAST

For his three kids
Late into the Philadelphia night,
Pop chalked happy scenes
On the kitchen chalk board.

In the morning,
While spooning Cheerios and
Sipping Ovaltine, we marveled
At Pop's farms with
Chickens, cows, pigs,
Mules, goats and sheep,
Under a smiling sun.

On the radio we heard
Amazing tales of adultery
(whatever that was),
False religion, Communist hoards
And the Atomic Bomb finale
As predicted in Revelation:
"Behold I am coming soon,
Bringing my recompense...
Outside the gates will be dogs
And sorcerers" hollered
Rev. Carl McIntire,
National prophet.

"Will Jesus let our dog inside
The gates?" Bobby asked mom,
As she squeezed
Fresh orange juice and
Poured spoons of cod liver oil.

Mom said Trixie would be ok.

From her high chair
Ruthie snuck Trixie
A comforting snack.

> *There came forth little children from out*
> *of the city and mocked him...Go up thou bald head.*
>
> I KINGS 2:23

QUESTIONS
FOR
ELISHA

In Sunday School we kids
Learn of Elisha,
Celebrity prophet,
Hustling along on
God-business,
Glory shining off
His naked pate.

Bumps into 42
Little children who
Laugh at his shine.

Blushing,
(He thought the comb-over worked),
Elisha has God call down
Two wild she bears
To tear the children apart.

She bears Elisha?
Two?

Well at least these children
Had faces — 42 of them.

Can't take a joke,
Eh, chrome dome?

23

Dog is God
Spelled backwards.
Or God is Dog.
Same thing.

A cliché
I don't care.

Or God is Love
Or Love is God,

LULU

So many words.

My old mutt Lulu
Had no words.
Her gaze,
Infinite love.

"Are you God?"
I asked into
Her eyes.

She didn't answer.

In photographs I still look
Into her eyes.
Still ask.

She still
Doesn't answer.

Have nothing to do with that innocent man...
In a dream last night I suffered much on account of him.

MATTHEW 27:19

Maybe I saw him long ago
In a crowd of priests
Yelling at Pontius.
The man was short,
Hard to see.

QUESTIONS FOR MRS. PILATE

At dinner Pontius wondered
Why all the fuss about
That little guy.

We had it pretty good back then
Except for the long commute
From Caesare to Jerusalem.

At Passover there were big
Crowds to celebrate the killing
Of Egyptian children.

Always the killing!
Was that the reason the little guy
Was so upset and
Turned over the temple tables?
Those poor animals —
Doves, lambs, calves,
Blood everywhere
To please their god.

Brave, the Jew was
In my dream, and

Young like Pontius once.
I adored him,
I was fourteen when
He took me.

Then Pontius got the job
Running Judea, Samaria, and Idumaea,
A real plum.
But when he paraded
The Emperor's Emblem into
Their cities, people got upset.
To save his job Pontius had to
Crucify 100,000 of them.

In my dream I passed the Jew
On the street and walked
Right on by: Ordinary he was,
But he said things nobody
Was saying like blessed are
The meek, the peacemakers,
The mourners, the merciful,
A whole laundry list.

He said not to care about
Money, and not to judge and
To love your enemies.

"Obviously a nobody,"
Said Pontius, right up to
His suicide.

But the nobody loved me.
Was it my fault
I loved him back?

Pop curled up in bed
And went to heaven
So quietly she
Didn't know he'd left
Without her.

Years later, dying,
She told me:"I am going
To find daddy."

MOM

At the hospital
Her minister hyped her trip:
"Dorothy, you are going on
A great adventure!"
Mom burped at the news,
"Excuse me," she apologized,
Polite to the end.

She delayed her
Great adventure for weeks.
Drowning in fluids,
Cancer everywhere.
She didn't want to leave
Her three kids.
"Dying is no joke," she joked.

Finally one night
Awash in morphine,
She set out to find Pop,
Certain he waited for her
In a place beyond all understanding.

Progress Is Our Most Important Project.
GENERAL ELECTRIC

For decades Pop labored
Under General Electric
Helping produce "Progress"
(The best idea they could come up with)
Keeping his Jesus idea private.

PROGRESS

In my 12th summer,
Pop, on vacation from GE,
Reshingled our summer house.
I climbed the ladder with him,
Nailed asbestos shingles
Dizzy from vertigo.

Beneath us frantic traffic
Concerned itself with holiday matters,

We were men working together
Doing the necessary work of shelter,
Up there nearer God's eye.

Late 1940's
Peach fuzz wonder
Fishing with Pop
On Great Egg Harbor,
Ocean City, N.J.

I spear live minnows
On my hooks, right up
Through their tiny backs.
They scream in voices
I can't hear,
Don't care anyway,
Because minnows
Catch flounders.

PUBERTY

Pop,
At the boat's bow,
Uses frozen clam bait,
Won't hurt living beings,
Any at all,
Won't prune a tree.
Catches no flounders.

Wishy washy
I laugh at him.
Flounder King, I am.
Pubic Master of the Seas.

Now,
Master of not much.
I want to scramble to
Gentle Pop
At the bow
But he has drifted away.

Be fruitful and multiply...all the animals birds and fish will live in fear of you.
GENESIS 1:28

QUESTIONS
FOR GOD

OK
We fear you
And your creatures
Fear us.
Neat plan.

We have been fearing
And multiplying
For eons.

We call ourselves
"Consumers."

We are eight billion.
We have obliterated
Elephants, tigers, fish
Plants, bugs etc.
Plus a good chunk of the air
Waters and forests, etc.

Everything fears us.
Now what?

Brother Constantine,
Was that cross just
The handle of your
Raised sword?

Maybe you were
Stoned? Drunk?
Blinded by the sun
In 313 A.D?

"In hoc signo vinces!"
You hollered and charged

Obliterated that
Other fellow,
Max somebody.

Into the future,
Full tilt boogie
For Christos,
Togas swirling
Pax Romanos Christos

Your Council of Nicaea —
Good call.
Straightened things out.
God and Christos are One.
Our guys,
Our Guy!

But did you have to murder
Your wife, kids, all
Those heathen?
Maybe clear that up?

But let's rejoice
You squeezed in a baptism
Just before you passed on
To glory, sin free.

Three hundred years
Outside the Empire!
Nero made torches of us.
You got us inside overnight:
Now our true light
Shines for all:

Sine qua non,
Oh, Corporate Grandfather!

THE END IS NEAR

I miss the smiling guy
On the corner of
42nd and 8th with his
"End Is Near" sign.

Gone to the internet,
I guess.

Empty faces everywhere now
At the corner of
42nd and 8th.

"This is a tough sermon,"
Said the young minister.
"Maybe the children should
Leave the pews for
Age appropriate activities."

None of us did,
Preferring to work on our
Biblical coloring books.

VISITING
MINISTER

"Ok then," he hurried on,
"You see Abram wants to sacrifice
Isaac, his only son, to the Lord.
No big deal in those days,
Everybody was into it,
Animals, kids, I mean God
Did it to Jesus.
So up the hill they go
'What's up Dad?' Isaac asks.
Abram readies his knife.
Presto a ram appears!
Stuck in a bush.
Dad kills the ram instead.
Whew! Close call eh kids?"

No answer from us kids,
Frantically coloring our books.

"Amen" said the minister.
Sat down as if shot.

Jesus died for our sins.
1 CORINTHIANS 15:3

"We are all sinners," announced
The bland Sunday school teacher.

"I'm no sinner" said I.
"You too, Billy."

SINNERS

What was the use then
Of being "Good,"
As Pop commanded.

Why the perfect dangle of
Sunday School attendance pins
On my sports jacket?

At least I was better
Than those doomed Catholic kids
Shamelessly dragging their rafts
To the beach on Sunday morning
After Mass.
"No beach on Sunday" Pop reminded me.

So at least I was better
Than those kids.
Jesus had a lot more
Dying to do for them
Than for me.

POP'S POEM

Pop said:
"The more you know
The more you know you
Don't know."

T.S. Eliot said:
"All our knowledge brings us
Nearer to our ignorance...
Where is the wisdom we
Have lost in knowledge?"

Pop never read poetry.
Didn't write it either.
Electricity was his calling.

But Pop's three lines
Sort of rhyme.

Eliot's don't.
And he used more words
To get there.

He was a good man.
JOB 1:1

STIGMATA

Job was a good man
And God gave him boils.
I was a good kid
And God gave me pimples.

Distained by leaping cheerleaders
I was surely loved by God.

God often afflicts those
He loves, said Rev McIntire.

A red face oozing pus
Was His test of my faith, I hoped.
Sort of like the stigmata of St. Francis,
To mix a metaphor about
Mixed signals from
He who loved me.

QUESTIONS FOR CHRISTIANS

Nailing him up was
The easy part.
Resigned he was,
Crying for his father.
Went quick.
Tossed him in a pile
With the other Jews.

But up he popped!
Resurrected his rebels said,
Walking about, still insisting
On love, forgiveness and such.

You Christians trashed lots of that,
John's drama said he
Was a temple whipper;
Revelation stuck him
In a bloody pantheon.

Your CEO Constantine removed
His own wife and kids
With the cross as his sign.

Next guys in funny dresses and
Fancy hats, with deep pockets
And loads of rules,
Made up stuff about his mom
And buried him in crusades.

But up he popped again!
Francis wandered here and there
Loving love, forgiving,
Healing, poor, joyous,
Doomed by the Big Hats.

But again, up he popped!
Luther, Calvin et. al.
Gave exhumation a go,
But buried him in a
Slew of words.

And on to Life Coach,
Sales Wizz,
Financial Guru,
TV Super Star,
Almost time for his
Official obituary.

Today he's really dead:
A pill for pain,
Porn for love,
Facebook for hugs,
The internet for wisdom.

Nobody gives a damn.
What are you going
To do about it?

**CHRISTIAN
SOLDIERS**

Because Pop was born in 1901
He missed his Christian duty
In WWI and WWII.
Lucky for him because
Christians were split about
Which flag Jesus would fly
In each tussle.

In WWI a Yale Divinity Professor
Saw Jesus "sighting down a
Gun barrel and running a bayonet
Through an enemy's body."
(Pop was too young for that one.)

In WWII Germany's church worthies
Proclaimed "Hitler was sent to us
By God...a swastika on our breasts,
A cross on our hearts."
(Pop was too old for that one.)

On 2003, born again Christian
George W. Bush butchered thousands
Of Iraqi innocents for a lie.
(Pop was dead).

My gentle father dodged a bullet.

They packaged Debby's
Cancer-free remains
with her Bible
In a lovely jug.

On a winter afternoon
She sat on a pedestal
Next to the graves of
Our Protestant parents.

FUNERAL

A Monsignor read his official
Words about dying etc.
Left out her 22 years as a shell.
Then hustled to his car.

"Monsignor!" I hollered.
Gave chase, caught him.
Drizzle on our faces.

"Monsignor, about the eucharist,
Is that really Jesus in
The bread and wine?"

He nodded, ducked into his car,
Tore off,
Windshield wipers thrashing
Violently.

How bizarre, I thought.
How wonderful.

PERMANENT RECORDS

Santa Claus kept a
Permanent Record,
Knew if you were
Naughty or nice.

So did Peter Rabbit
At Easter.

The school principal
Kept a Permanent Record,
Let your parents know
What was on it.

And God kept the Permanent Record
Of all Permanent Records.

The point of all the records
Was for me
To stay the heck
Out of hell.

I was born on
Philadelphia's Main Line.
A railroad hacked out by
Robber Barons
Who planted it
With estates and
Enshrined their names in
A Blue Book,
Still kept up to date
By society Presbyterians.

BLUE BOOKS

Jesus was spawned on
David's Main Line.
A bit confusing is
The Jesus Blue Book.
Whores Tamar and Rahab
Made the cut.
Rahab is Boaz's mom
Who married Ruth and
Down the line
To Jesus. Except
Joseph steps aside
For God.

But why quibble?
At Bryn Mawr Presbyterian
Jesus's Blue Book and
The Main Line Blue Book
Merged in the switchyards of
Our souls.

The oxen stumbled and Ussah reached out.
2ND SAMUEL 6:7

QUESTIONS
FOR
UZZAH'S DAD

Uzzah's Pop told him:
"God loves a cheerful giver.
Be helpful and you
Will go far."

But when King David's
Ox tripped and
The Holy Ark tipped,
Almost toppled
From the cart,
Uzzah reached out,
Tried to save it,
Touched the sacred.

And got God-smoted.

He let his seed spill on the ground.
GENESIS 38:9

SELF ABUSE
1955

Boys
My name is Onan and
I got a bum rap.

Onanism,
Say the preachers,
Is a nasty sin.
Not so.
Here's the truth on
The jisim ism.

God liquidated my brother,
Told me to bed his wife,
Have his kids.

I don't feel like it.
Coitus Interuptus for me.
(Latin talk, don't ask.)

So God flushed me too.
Unfair! I was spilling,
Not wacking!

Your preachers are
Spinning the spawning.
So wack until your cock flops!
But make sure the door locks
And the toilet paper plops.

Thank you for letting me
Clear my name.

At Debby's wake
Her nurse announced
That she prayed the Rosary
every day.

"Don't know much about
Church rules,
Don't much care.
Just the rosary and
The number 27!"
She sobbed.

27

Her son dead at 27,
Swerved his motorcycle
To miss a possum
On March 27.

Her theology:
27 this
27 that.

Every hour he
Contacted his mom
In the number 27.

"I live near Rt. 27,"
I offered.

"You see!"
She spilled her wine,
Clutched my arm hard.

In Bob's sunny backyard.

No authority exists without God's permission.
ROMANS 13:1

KINDERGARTEN
THEOLOGY

Mrs Hotchkiss was appointed
By God
To be our kindergarten teacher.

"If you kids don't stop yelling
The ceiling will fall on you!"
She yelled.
If that didn't do it,
The Stuff,
(Something in a brown jar),
Did.

If she slathered the Stuff
On your mouth, you couldn't
Eat or drink forever.

One day she dragged
Loudmouth Chucky Higgins
To her Stuff closet.
And slowly unscrewed the lid.

Smiling, slowly unscrewing,
While Chuck pissed a puddle.

Always smiling.

Something bad happened to my
Kid's theology that day.
The smile did it.

And the Lord said unto Satan,
Hast thou considered my servant Job?
JOB 2:3

Right about here
In Debby's Bible
We find Job

Good fellow,
Few sins,

GAMBLER   Rich.

God tortured him
To win a bet with
The Devil.

Then God fixed him
Up again
Having won his bet.

And Debby?
Kind Debby?

Her ashes got crammed
Into a designer jug.

At least Job got
His stuff back.

The free gift of God is eternal life in Jesus Christ
ROMANS 6:23

GETTING
SAVED

In the spring of 1949,
Rev. McIntire demanded:
"Put your hands on the radio,
Say you believe, and
Be saved."
I did.

In the summer of 1949,
Billy Graham ordered me
To raise my hand at his rally.
And get saved "Do it now. Hell
awaits you!"
I did.

At vacation Bible school
A frantic high school girl,
Our stick ball instructor,
Hollered:"Kneel in the sand and
Accept Jesus as your personal savior."
I did.

That winter I told
Neighborhood kids to
 Circle their sleds
Bow their heads
And accept Jesus.
They did.

Having no other business,
We started a snowball fight
And played without ceasing.

He cried with a loud voice, Lazarus come! out!
JOHN 11:43

He was a vicious turtle,
Softshelled, long snouted,
Ugly, ate anything.
I bought him for a quarter
And thought he was immortal.

TURTLE   When he died suddenly
Pop carried him to his
Homebuilt electric generator
And attached wires to his paws.

Pop cranked mightily and
The turtle shivered and shook
With jolts of homemade energy.
But Lazarus he was not.

It was the first time
Pop and I met death together.

Even Pop's huge tenderness
Couldn't bring him back.

QUESTIONS
FOR
ST. AUGUSTINE:
"JUST WAR"
JESUS?

Is it not so that
On or about 397 AD
You announced your
Theology of "Just War?"
Is it not also correct that
You spun that notion from
Parables about the Lord's
Feast: "Compel" became
"Force?"

Is it not also true that
The following events
(A partial list)
Were spun by your
Just War musings?

The murder of 1,500 Jews
In Worms, Speier and Manz (1096)?

The slaughter of non-Latin faithful
"Babies roasted on spits,"
In Peter the Hermit's crusade (1101)?

The exterminations of Constantople:
Eastern orthodox nuns raped,
The sacraments ravaged,
A prostitute proclaiming from
The Patriarch's throne (1204)?

The liquidation of the Waldensians
Because their barefoot holiness
Mocked the Pope's glory (1179)?

The elimination of 15,000
Christian Cathari
"Showing mercy to neither
Order, sex or age." (1209)?

And onward to Torquemada,
"Gott Mit Uns"
And In God We Trust?"

Or have we somehow
Not understood your
Just War spin,
Oh Hero of Hippo?

MICAH

Buried deep
In Debby's Bible
We find Micah:
"What does God
Require of you,
But to do justice,
Love kindness,
And walk humbly
With your God."

Can't spin that.
Now we are getting
Somewhere
Among her.
Ashes.

PRAYING

Sundays at church
We all prayed for world peace
And for the saving of billions
Of hellbound heathen.

All week Pop prayed to Jesus
While driving his Chevy from
Job site to job site for GE.
He was a low voltage engineer
Responsible for industrial repair.
On the Chevy's radio
Evangelists prayed mightily
With him.
At dinner our family prayed
Thanks for the food and
We each recited Bible verses,
My favorite was
"Wine is a mocker
Strong drink is raging."
It pleased Pop.
His dad had been a drunk.

At bedtime, Mom heard
My prayers: "God bless
My turtles, snakes and frogs
And my dog Trixie, my cat Boots,
And mother and dad and
Bob and Ruth and
President Eisenhower
And may Mr. Stalin see
The light of Jesus."

Then she kissed me goodnight.
And in the arms of a gentle God
I lay me down to sleep.

50'S MEDIA

Howdy Doody
Was a good guy,
A TV puppet with
A wooden Christian smile.

Mr. Bluster stormed
Into Howdy's show
With a wooden, Satanic scowl.

Rev. McIntire,
Radio evangelist, screeched:
"For the love of Jesus
Atom bomb the Godless Reds
Before they bomb us!"
On Pop's Philco.

Like Howdy,
I kept on smiling.

And he shall be burned with fire.
REVELATION 18:8

**BILLY'S
BONER**

Hell was big in
Billy Graham's sermons.
Loving me, Billy
Warned that any second
I could die and
End up like this:
"The little child is in
The red hot oven.
Hear how it screams
To come out,
See how it turns and twists
Itself about in the fire.
It beats its head against
The roof of the oven.
It stamps its little feet
On the floor." *

Years later I toured
A New York S&M club,
Witnessed loving care
Displayed in inventive tortures.

Did Billy sprout a boner
While ranting so lovingly?
Heck I didn't even know what
A boner was in 1950.

* Rev. Joseph Furniss
The Sight of Hell
1807

"So there you have it,"
The Expert said:
"Father, Son, Holy Ghost."

The Father should be hauled before
The International Court of Justice
For Unpeakable Crimes.
(Probably plead paranoia, anxiety,
Manic depression, etc.)

TRINITY

Son tried to fix it up
With Unspeakable Love.

Holy Spirit moves among us
With Unspeakable Sweetness.

That's two votes
Out of three.

Veto proof.

Whoever hits his father or his mother
is to be put to death.

EXODUS 21:15

In 1916,
Pop's booze sodden dad
Dragged his mom down
A Philadelphia street and
Pop slugged him.

THE STONING

He just, he just
Hauled off and slammed him
"Hard in the stomach,"
Ran away to a neighbor's house,
Hid for days, waiting for
His stoning.

Decades later Pop got it.
His son, a fancy teen agnostic,
Stoned him with doubts
About all that
Pop had lived for.

FAITH HEALER

Oral Roberts was Pop's TV doctor.
Oral prayed while
Pop held his bulging hernia
With one hand,
The other on the TV antenna,
As instructed by Oral.

For years,
Pop waited,
Kept the faith.

Maybe that's why Mom,
When Oral asked "Sister"
To send funds for his
Worldwide ministry, sighed
"I'm not your sister,"
And tore up his letter
Into tiny pieces that
Fluttered on the formica
Like funeral flowers.

*Your love for me was wonderful, passing
the love of women.*
SAMUEL 1:26

DAVID
FOR
SUNDAY
SCHOOL

Upstart David,
Mooning over the King's son.

"Well, Jon's not available"
Roars King Saul,
"But the girl goes for
100 Philistine foreskins."

"Done!" laughs David,
And delivers 200 foreskins!
Terrifies Dad,
Hooks up with his daughter.

Saul consults a witch about
This horny kid.
"Bad news!" says the witch,
"The Kid is
The new King!"

So many lessons for us
Teen Sunday Schoolers
About foreskins and celebrity.
The Kid wacked Goliath
With a few pebbles and a homemade
Slingshot. So easy to make
A name for yourself.
And The Kid gets to be
The great, great, great etc.
Grandaddy of Jesus ...
Well sort of, but that's
A private matter between
Joseph and Mary.
And The Kid was a published poet
A switch-hitting Renaissance Man!
All those Psalms he wrote,
Well for sure number 18,
But hey he got his byline
On a stack of them.
And what about Bathsheba
Bathing for The Kid's binoculars?
A wacker's dream!
I'd have killed her husband too...
Bathsheba, wet and glistening
In the noon sun...
Actually it was a girl in
An outdoor shower,
Ocean City, N.J. 1954.

Eunuchs for the Kingdom of God.
MATTHEW 19:12

The leaping cheerleaders
Were driving me crazy,
Origen.

In Sunday School I heard
You knocked off your gonads
For God.

QUESTIONS
FOR
ORIGEN,
200 AD

What I needed to know was
How to proceed?

A razor?
A knife?
A rope on a slammed
Door knob?

After praying silently
On his knees
By his bed,
Pop died in his sleep.

"Jesus gently took him
Home, that sweet, sweet man,"
I wailed, alone in the attic
After a canned funeral,
Attended by few.

SILENCE

Mom said afterward:
"He died of a broken heart,"
Meaning Bob consulting a
Godless shrink and
Me cavorting in Paris
With wine and loose women.

Pop hadn't said much
About cavorting and shrinks.
He let Jesus say it all.

In my dream that night
Pop drives up to our house
In his old Chevy,
Home from work,
Lightning! A resurrection!
He hugs us all.

Then I notice
His mouth is sealed
With duct tape.

TEETH

What amazes me
About TV evangelists
Is their teeth

Who's your dentist?
I want to ask them.
All heaven must gleam
From your perfect shine.

Son, do what your father tells you.
PROVERBS 6:29

**GOD'S
FINGERTIPS**

At the open winter window
I reached out for help
In the night sky,
Hoping He'll touch my
Fingertips.

Nothing worked with
This being a good Christian boy.
I was banned by
The entire teen world.

Nearby, born-again Pop
Watched me reaching
"Ah cut that out Bill,"
He said.

LEGAL TENDER: THE LATERAN PALACE

In 1200 AD a nation's riches
Were tallied in holy snippets
Of the saints and shreds
Of this and that:
The heads of Peter and Paul,
The Ark of the Covenant,
The Tablets of Moses,
The Rod of Aaron,
An Urn of Manna,
The Virgin's Tunic,
The Hair Shirt of John The Baptist,
The Last Super Dining Table,
The foreskin of Jesus.

Today we tally computer blips.
What are you banking on?

QUESTIONS FOR THE DEVIL

Debby was a Jewish-Catholic.
Did she make the cut?

Brother Bob never read her Bible.
Will he join her?

My sister Ruth is an Orthodox Jew.
I suspect she will be with you.

Is Pop there?
He never ate Jesus.

Is Mom there?
She said Pop was too religious.

What about billions of little kids
Who never heard of you?

Where do you find room for them,
Enough matches?

What does it say about us Christians
That we adore your Boss?

For Mom,
After Pop died suddenly
There was Heaven.

For the uncle,
An engineer in the
Thermostat business and
An atheist in the
Reason business,
There was Science.

SCIENCE

"Why didn't you get him
A shot of adrenalin?"
He demanded of my sobbing
Mother, as his brother's body
Lay cooling on the bed.
As if Mom enabled the
Heart attack with her
Ridiculous, sloppy
Faith.

As if Science solved
Everything.

As if that was all
The condolence he knew
How to offer.

TWO RINGS

At Sunday School graduation
The minister handed me
An engraved, silver plated
"I Am His" ring.
IAH I was branded.

In Junior High School
The ring disappeared
Into my sock drawer,
To emerge again when
I needed a trinket
To impress a girlfriend.

"Ahh" she gasped,
Bewildered when I pushed
It onto her finger.

The ring soon disappeared
When she did.

For years I didn't miss
The I Am His ring.
I bought a new one on
The boardwalk for 25 cents.
I named it "The Ring of Myself"
Although I had no idea who
That self might be.

Now I miss that IAH ring,
Wherever it is,
In whoever's sock drawer.

DEVOTION

For decades Simon Stylites
Slept on a wooden perch
Atop a sixty foot pole.
Downward he preached about
The salvation in suffering.

For decades my brother
Slept on a wooden floor
Next to his wife's shell.
Did not preach.

Simon got a church built
Over his pole.

Bob got to watch tv
Alone.

"I'm tearing down the Truth
Block by block and
I'll build it up again
Block by block."
Bragged Teen Wizz.

"That's nice," the girl smiled.
Kept her pants on.

"But where, Oh Teen Wizz,
After reading *Philosophy Made Simple*
From Aristotle to Zarathustra,
Did you find your first blocks?"

"Love your God,
Love your neighbor
As yourself."

"Good call, kid.
If you don't know that,
Don't even bother
Playing with blocks."

QUESTIONS FOR JOHN ON PATMOS

John, John,
Christian John!
You've been too long
Alone on that island.

Did you know that
Nero is history,
Domitian will be soon?
Revenge is the Lord's,
Remember?

And isn't your Revelation
About the 666 beast,
And the lamb with seven horns
And seven eyes, and
The four horsemen and
The seven-headed dragon
A bit over the top?

My daughter's Dr. Seuss books
said it better.

And John,
Christian John,
It's all been said before:
The psalmist sang:
"A blessing on him who
Seizes your babies and
Dashes them against the rocks."

That should be enough violence,
John. Old news is no news.
No reason to get yourself
All worked up.
You are centuries late to
The ancient slaughter.

Enjoy your island, John.
Can you remember that
Jesus loves you?

Fleeing the chattering mourners,
Alone in the dark attic,
On an old rolled rug,
I was Pop's baby again,
A child of the child of God.

"You know it all now, Pop!"
I called to him in heaven.

OLD RUG

Unmarried at 37, he had worried
In a letter to Mom:
"Luke says men and women who
Are worthy to rise from the dead
Will not marry."

Mom countered with Mark:
"A man shall leave his father
And mother and be joined to his wife."

Pop bought her blandishments,
Left his parents' house and
Took a chance on eternity.

That's why I sat on the rug
Wailing to him.
Unless of course Luke was right
And he wasn't there.

Memo to My Lord Pope Honorius III
From Father Flavius
Re: Relics
October 3, 1226

ST FRANCIS

Holy Father,
It has come to my attention
That Francis of Assisi,
Who obscenely professes
To follow the Naked Christ,
Is dying.

Blind, in deserved agony,
Slathered in sores
That his followers boast
Are Christ's stigmata,
He lies alone in a reed hut
Of the kind preferred by his ilk.

In his final delirium
He continues to bless the poor
And decry our wealth,
Loving his Lady Poverty
And thus blaspheming our own Lady.

His suffering is welcome,
And from God,
Considering what slander
He has unleashed on us,
Holy Father.

However, after studying
the demographics of the matter
May I suggest an opportunity
To propagate the faith
Around this troublesome gnat?

Francis has a gigantic self-regard.
He brags he is an instrument of
God's peace, that he is
In love with love.
He has stirred up a rowdy rabble
With his strutting showmanship.
Thousands have adopted his slovenly style
Of tunic, rope belt and cowl.
These multitudes tramp
The highways barefoot
Singing and praying and preaching
Without our permission,
And women among them.

Therein lies our opportunity.
We can use their devotion and
Their need to hold onto him.
His corpse, divided into teeth and
Bone and hair and nails,
Well packaged and distributed
As relics throughout the world
Would raise considerable sums
For our treasury.

With some of that profit
We could erect a handsome basilica
Over what remains of his corpse

In short,
As soon as he is gone to hell
(Which may be any day now),
We must obtain his body
By whatever means,
And parcel out relics
To the rabble.

Plus, of course, his basilica
Will prove profitable
For the pilgrimage trade,
After we declare him to be
A Saint.

In this manner,
Francis will pay back holy church
For all the troubles
He has inflicted on us,
And Your Holiness.

MORNING AFTER

The Holy Spirit drifts in
On little fog feet.

One morning I wake up
And she's right there
Beside me.

I don't know
How she got there
Or what her name is.

She rolls over and
Whispers in my ear.

"Try to remember."

Summertime. Maine.
A cabin I built with
A hammer, saw, trisquare,
On a thick concrete slab,
Two by six studs,
Solid. Confident.

GRACE

Our daughter, age six,
Bouncing on her bed,
Bangs her head hard on
The pine wall
I nailed there.

At the Island Clinic,
The doctor worries about
A blood clot in her brain,
Orders an emergency CAT Scan
At a hospital up the coast.

Lily sobbing on the back seat,
Me? If she dies
I will die with her.
Nothing more certain.

Doing eighty miles an hour,
Panicked, suicidal,
On twisting roads,
And this thing happens.

The blueberry fields ignite
With love for our child
For all the living and dying,
For every creature of God.

Grace transcends us,
Infuses every pebble,
As we tear desperately
North to Damascus.
And I see Him plain.

"Cancer" the oncologist
Quietly announces.
Surgery, chemo, radiation etc.
"A fighting chance."

PARK AVENUE

Wandering out of her office
Down Park Avenue,
I come to an immense church,
Stumble up the steps into
A rapture of Marble,
Stained glass,
Looming organ,
Velvet cushioned pews,
Immortal slabs of thanks
For wealthy dead donors.

I duck under the pew,
Shut my eyes,
Block it out,
I find Him whom
I am seeking.

Rock of Ages cleft for me.
Let me hide myself in thee.
Rock of Ages

**THE
CLEFT**

That's the place
For a politician,
In the cleft.

Tell the people
You are with Him
In the cleft.

Ignore pesky Jesus
Just get into
His cleft.

Whatever your racket,
Church, state, corporate,
There's votes
In the cleft.
Hide yourself.

NEIGHBORS

Our family was Presbyterian.
John Calvin was our founder,
A theocrat. He said his
Trinity idea was non-negotiable,
And so was predestination and
Others of his notions.

One didn't contradict Calvin.
Michael Servetus did in 1553.
It ended badly for him.

In the 1940's we kept
An eye on the Jews down the hill,
The Catholics next door.
The divorced Methodist nearby.

We knew where they lived.
They were special.
We were nice to them.
Neighbors.

QUESTIONS
FOR
MARTIN LUTHER

Martin,
What did your
Sola Scriptura
Have to offer
That the Pope's outfit
Didn't?

Sure the indulgences
Were outrageous,
The priests
Lived big on the pig.

But where in your
Messy Word of God
Can you find God?

You removed the Pope,
But up popped
Everybody else!
Iconoclasts,
Anabaptists
Witchburners,
Rampaging peasants
Insane presidents.

Jesus will forgive you
Martin.
You meant well.

At church, my turn to read
The lesson from my beat up Bible,
(Presented to Billy, Oak Park
Sunday School, Philadelphia, 1949).

I recite that David defeats
The Moabites, executes two out of
Three prisoners face down in dirt
And praises the God we worship.

LIAM

Afterwards I float from the bleeding
Altar, wondering what I am doing
Back here among the bloody Christians
Of my childhood,

A seven year old spirit,
Little suffering Liam the epileptic,
Appears from the pews.
A football helmet on his head,
His protection from daily seizures.

Liam hugs my knees hard.
Wordless.

I toss the Bible in a pew.
Now I know what I am doing
Back here.

IN THE GARDEN

After a stock funeral
In the mighty Main Line church,
After a few gravesite clichés
From the minister,
And a quote from Ecclesiastes:
"A time to be born...
A time to die.." etc.
An electric jack powered Pop's body
Deep into the earth.

My eulogy,
My hymn to him,
Stayed in my pocket.
It was Pop's moment, I figured,
Best I shut up.

But I tell you
He wasn't a stock character
Out of .some suburban handbook.
He lived for Jesus, not for
Real estate, golf, cocktails
Proper cars and chemical lawns.

After the sober Presbyterian wake,
After the deluge of food, flowers
And equivocating well-wishers offering
"Whatever thoughts sustain you now..."
Mom and I walked in the crocus
Blooming garden.

"How come you are sad, Mom?"
I asked. "Pop's in heaven right?"
"Yes Daddy's seeing beautiful
Sights now. He's happy but
I am so lonely. I guess I'm
Just selfish."

She silenced me.

THE NEW APOSTLE'S CREED

Love

And

Wonder

Bill Henderson was born in Philadelphia, Pennsylvania in 1941. At the age of 10 he wrote his first poem. After college he lived in France for two years where he wrote his first novel in a Paris attic. The novel was rejected everywhere. So, four years after writing *The Kid That Could*, Bill published it himself.

Between 1971 and 1973 Bill served as an associate editor at Doubleday, then went on his own to found Pushcart Press. The first edition of the *Pushcart Prize* was published in 1976. Since 1973 he has edited dozens of titles for Pushcart Press, and is the author of six memoirs. His honors include The Ivan Sandrof Lifetime Achievement Award from the National Book Critics Circle in 2006 and A Distinguished Service To The Arts citation from The American Academy of Arts and Letters in 2020.

Bill and his wife Genie Chipps have one daughter, Lily. They divide their time between the East End of Long Island, where Bill is an Elder and occasional lay preacher at his local church, and Maine, where he is the proprietor of the world's smallest bookstore.